To My Grandson with Love

JEANETTE CHRISTY

ISBN 978-1-0980-3124-4 (paperback)
ISBN 978-1-0980-3125-1 (digital)

Copyright © 2020 by Jeanette Christy

All rights reserved. No part of this publication may be reproduced, distributed, or transmitted in any form or by any means, including photocopying, recording, or other electronic or mechanical methods without the prior written permission of the publisher. For permission requests, solicit the publisher via the address below.

Christian Faith Publishing, Inc.
832 Park Avenue
Meadville, PA 16335
www.christianfaithpublishing.com

Printed in the United States of America

Contents

Preface

When my son was a teenager, he asked me what his purpose was. I was not a Christian at the time and did not have an answer for him. I have watched him over the years deal with depression and suicidal thoughts, because life can be pretty hard sometimes. Today, I know what his purpose is, and so does he.

We have seen how God uses us to bring joy to others and to help others when they need it. God did not give us life so that we could use it for selfish reasons. When you let the Holy Spirit touch your soul, you change; it is like you can fly.

I felt the Holy Spirit touch my soul before I knew a word of scripture. It happened when my sister invited me to church, and we were singing praises to God and thanking Jesus for his sacrifice. I went from "It's all about me" to "It's all about what Jesus taught while on earth."

In 2018, our pastor gave the congregation a challenge. For seven consecutive days, we were to hand-write a prayer for our grandchildren and give it to them daily (hopefully to be saved). This book is a result of that challenge.

I pray that when your grandson wants to know his purpose, this book will help answer that question.

Blessings to you.

Jeanette Christy
Author, God's Faithful Servant

God's Masterpiece

"So God created people in His own image; God patterned them after Himself; male and female He created them." (Genesis 1:27, NLT)

God created the heavens and earth, and He also created you. As amazing as the heavens and earth are, you are His greatest masterpiece! There is not another like you, so thank God for giving you life and making you so AMAZING!

Prayer

Lord, *thank you for bringing my grandson into my life. What a blessing!*

Take Shelter in Times of Trouble

"The Lord Himself goes before you and will be with you; He will never leave you nor forsake you. Do not be afraid; do not be discouraged." (Deuteronomy 31:8, NIV)

As a storm approaches, take shelter in God's love and His promise to never leave you nor forsake you. He will help you weather the storm, then stay with you during life's journey.

Prayer

Lord, thank you for being so faithful, for keeping Your promises, and for loving my grandson as much as You do.

Lean with God

"Trust in the Lord with all your heart, and do not lean on your own understanding. In all your ways acknowledge Him, and He will make straight your paths." (Proverbs 3:5–6, NIV)

When taking a curve on a motorcycle, you need to lean with the bike. If you lean the other direction, you will lose your balance. It is the same way with God. Lean with Him, and you won't lose your balance.

Prayer

__Lord__, hold tight to my grandson and help him stay balanced. I pray he learns to trust in You completely, for You will provide everything he needs to live a well-balanced life.

Experience the Beauty

Jesus' Sermon on the Mount

"Therefore I tell you, do not worry about your life, what you will eat or drink; or about your body, what you will wear. Is not life more than food, and the body more than clothes? Look at the birds of the air; they do not sow or reap or store away in barns, and yet your heavenly Father feeds them. Are you not much more valuable than they? Can any one of you by worrying add a single hour to your life?" (Matthew 6:25–27, NIV)

There's a saying: "If God can take a caterpillar and turn it into a beautiful butterfly, think what He can do with you." I already see the beautiful person you are, but when you put your trust in God, He enlightens your inner beauty.

Prayer

Lord, please help my grandson experience the inner beauty and peace that comes with knowing You.

Be Part of a Team

"And this is His commandment: We must believe in the name of His Son, Jesus Christ, and love one another, just as He commanded us. Those who obey God's commandments live in fellowship with Him, and He with them. And we know He lives in us because the Holy Spirit lives in us." (1 John 3:23–24, NLT)

Working together as a team definitely has its advantages. When you share the responsibilities equally, everyone wins. God's got an awesome team. All you have to do is ask to be on it.

Prayer

Lord, *I'm asking that my grandson be called onto Your team—You, God, Your Son, Jesus, and the Holy Spirit and my grandson would make AN AWESOME TEAM!*

Let Your Light Shine

Jesus' Sermon on the Mount

"You are the light of the world. A town built on a hill cannot be hidden. Neither do people light a lamp and put it under a bowl. Instead they put it on its stand, and it gives light to everyone in the house. In the same way, let your light shine before others, that they may see your good deeds and glorify your Father in heaven." (Matthew 5:14–16, NIV)

You are indeed a ray of sunshine in my life; you light it up! Jesus is the light of the world; let Him be your light. When you live as Jesus taught, your light will shine, and you will feel such peace.

Prayer

Lord, *thank you for sending Your Son, Jesus, to teach us the way to live a righteous life. I pray my grandson experiences such joy in knowing You.*

Choose a Path

"The Lord is my shepherd, I lack nothing. He makes me lie down in green pastures, He leads me beside quiet waters, He refreshes my soul. He guides me along the right paths for His name's sake. Even though I walk through the darkest valley, I will fear no evil, for You are with me; Your rod and Your staff, they comfort me." (Psalm 23:1–4, NIV)

A boulder in the river never stops the river; it just sends the water in two different directions. Many times in life, you will come to a "boulder in the river" or a "fork in the road" and have to make a decision. Ask God for guidance before deciding.

Prayer

Lord, *please guide my grandson in making the right decisions when he comes to a boulder in the river of life.*

Feel the Passion

"This is the day the Lord has made; let us rejoice and be glad in it." (Psalm 118:24, NIV)

There is excitement in life, and whether it is snow-boarding, playing music, doing missionary work, teaching, or anything else, do it with passion. Live each day to the fullest, because it is a gift from God.

Prayer

Lord, thank You for Your Son, Jesus, who has so much passion. I pray that my grandson will experience such passion in his lifetime.

Get Back Up

"Have not I commanded you? Be strong and courageous. Do not be frightened and do not be dismayed, for the Lord your God is with you wherever you go." (Joshua 1:9, NIV)

Life has a way of knocking you down, but when you have God on your side, you can get back up. Trust God to be there, even when you think you don't need Him, because He never stops loving you.

Prayer

Lord, *please help my grandson realize that You will always be there for him.*

Feel the Power

"For the Spirit God gave us does not make us timid, but gives us power, love and self-discipline." (2 Timothy 1:7, NIV)

Like a large wave, you can have an awesome amount of power and at the same time be calming. Your heart is big, and I love being around you! Find a way to use your power for good.

Prayer

Lord, *please show my grandson the way to use his power in a positive way to help others and do Your work.*

Fly Proud with Friends

"One who has unreliable friends soon comes to ruin, but there is a friend who sticks closer than a brother." (Proverbs 18:24, NIV)

Your personality is like a kite. It is fun, it is some-times uncontrollable but always fascinating. Be careful, for like the kite, you can be carried away and sent crashing. Choose your friends carefully, because they too can send you crashing.

Prayer

Lord, *please help my grandson to make good decisions regarding friends and actions. Let him fly proud in Your love.*

Help One Another

"In everything I did, I showed you that by this kind of hard work we must help the weak, remembering the words the Lord Jesus Himself said: 'It is more blessed to give than to receive.'" (Acts 20:35, NIV)

Every once in a while, you will come across someone who needs help. Lend a helping hand through the kindness of your heart and expect nothing in return.

Prayer

Lord, *I ask that you touch my grandson's heart so that when he sees someone in need, he will find a way to help them.*

Rise Up

"We have different gifts, according to the grace given to each of us. If your gift is prophesying, then prophesy in accordance with your faith; if it is serving, then serve; if it is teaching, then teach; if it is to encourage, then give encouragement; if it is giving, then give generously; if it is to lead, do it diligently; if it is to show mercy, do it cheerfully." (Romans 12:6–8, NIV)

I can't express enough the importance of rising up to your God-given talents. You are fantastic in God's eyes (mine too), so find what you are good at and put your heart into it, and don't forget to thank God for your talents.

Prayer

Lord, *please help my grandson to realize his God-given talents and use them to help others.*

Don't Get Swept Away

"On the last and greatest day of the festival, Jesus stood and said in a loud voice, 'Let anyone who is thirsty come to me and drink. Whoever believes in me, as Scripture has said, rivers of living water will flow from within them.'" (John 7:37–38, NIV)

Life is like a waterfall. It is easy to get caught up in the ever-moving moments of life, and like the river leading to the falls, you can get swept away. Be careful not to get swept away by things that are not pleasing to God.

Prayer

Lord, *please help my grandson make good choices and not get swept away. I pray that he seeks Your love, believes in Jesus as his savior, and is touched by the Holy Spirit.*

Find Joy in the Climb

"I know what it is to be in need, and I know what it is to have plenty. I have learned the secret of being content in any and every situation, whether well fed or hungry, whether living in plenty or in want. I can do all this through Him who gives me strength." (Philippians 4:12–13, NIV)

I understand life can be a little intimidating, but you need to know you are loved by God, by your family, and by others. As Paul wrote, you need to be content in any situation as you climb the steps of life. You will find contentment and joy when walking with God.

Prayer

***Lord**, please take my grandson's hand and walk with him as he climbs the steps of life. May he find contentment and joy in knowing You.*

Be Forgiving

Jesus' Sermon on the Mount

"But to you who are listening I say:
Love your enemies, do good to those who
hate you, bless those who curse you, pray
for those who mistreat you. If someone
slaps you on one cheek, turn to them the
other also. If someone takes your coat, do
not withhold your shirt from them. Give to
everyone who asks you, and if anyone takes
what belongs to you, do not demand it back.
Do to others as you would have them do to
you." (Luke 6:27–31, NIV)

It seems that many young people today are being bullied. The truth of the matter is that those who bully are hurting on the inside; they don't feel loved. So if this happens to you, ask God for strength, pray for them, and forgive them.

Prayer

Lord, *I pray that my grandson, if bullied, will turn his heart to You and forgive those who have turned against him.*

Be Willing to Listen

"The end of a matter is better than its beginning, and patience is better than pride." (Ecclesiastes 7:8, NIV)

Sometimes we are so opinionated that we don't take time to listen to the other person's opinion. Listen, contemplate, ask God for guidance, and then make your well-thought-out opinion.

Prayer

Lord, *I pray that You give my grandson the patience to listen to others and to You before forming an opinion.*

Do Not Be Envious

"But the fruit of the Spirit is love, joy, peace, forbearance, kindness, goodness, faithfulness, gentleness and self-control. Against such things there is no law. Those who belong to Christ Jesus have crucified the flesh with its passions and desires. Since we live by the Spirit, let us keep in step with the Spirit. Let us not become conceited, provoking and envying each other." (Galatians 5:22–26, NIV)

It is so easy to envy those who have more than you, but you need to be content with what you have. Material things do not bring eternal satisfaction; they satisfy for only a moment, and then it is gone.

Prayer

Lord, *I pray that my grandson finds eternal satisfaction in knowing You and realizes how much You love him. Help him to be content and not envious.*

Be Slow to Anger

"My dear brothers and sisters, take
note of this: Everyone should be quick to
listen, slow to speak and slow to become
angry, because human anger does not pro-
duce the righteousness that God desires."
(James 1:19, NIV)

Anger is a hard emotion to control, especially today where road rage and violence is seen everywhere. But I can tell you when you feel anger coming on, just asked God to take over. All of a sudden, the anger goes away. It really is that easy.

Prayer

Lord, *I pray that during times in my grandson's life when he feels anger coming on, please fill his heart with Your love and bring him peace.*

Have Integrity

"For the Lord gives wisdom; from His mouth come knowledge and understanding; He stores up sound wisdom for the upright; He is a shield to those who walk in integrity... For wisdom will come into your heart, and knowledge will be pleasant to your soul." (Proverbs 2:6–7,10, ESV)

One of the hardest things in life to achieve is integrity. It means speaking the truth, even if it embarrasses us or that we may be rejected by others. It means keeping promises; if you say you will do something, then you need to do it. I have faith in you; you can do this with God's help.

Prayer

Lord, *I am asking you to instill character in my grandson that he will go through life with deep integrity.*

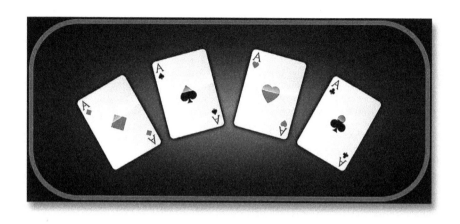

Start with a Great Foundation

Jesus' Sermon on the Mount

> "Therefore everyone who hears these words of mine and puts them into practice is like a wise man who built his house on the rock. The rain came down, the streams rose, and the winds blew and beat against that house; yet it did not fall, because it had its foundation on the rock." (Matthew 7:24–25, NIV)

In the game of Solitaire, the Ace is the foundation on which all other cards are placed. If the Ace represented your LOVE OF JESUS, then the game of life would end with THE KING.

Prayer

Lord, *I pray that my grandson starts with a great foundation by understanding Your love for him and, as he journeys through life, comes to love You in return.*

You are indeed a blessing!

*Insert a photo of you
and / or your grandson*

About the Author

Jeanette Christy is blessed to live in Northern Michigan with her husband, Jon. She is very active in her church and loves being surrounded by Christians. Since she has three teen grandsons and is concerned with the growing teen suicide rate in this country, she found it urgent that she reach out and try to connect with these teens through the love of God and their grandparents.